UPLIFTING POETRY TO
REJUVENATE THE HURTING SOUL

by

Rowena Smith

Uplifting Poetry To Rejuvenate The Hurting Soul

by

Rowena Smith

Copyright 2020 ICHAMPION Publishing

Published by iCHAMPION Publishing

P.O. Box 2352 Frisco, TX 75034

Content edit by Nikia Hammonds-Blakely and iCHAMPION Publishing

Library of Congress Cataloging-in-Publication Data Publisher and Printing by iCHAMPION Publishing

Poems Written By: Rowena Smith

Illustrated By: iCHAMPION Publishing

Cover Design By: Renee Huffman

ISBN: 978-1-7362684-0-7

Categories:

POETRY

INSPIRATION

My Beloved Rowena,

It has been a great honor and most definitely a privilege working with you over the years. Your service to the kingdom of God especially to our beloved leaders Archbishop Willie Bolden and Pastor Rhonda Bolden. Your Divine creativity and your spirit of excellence is priceless to mankind everywhere. I am so pleased that you have finally fulfilled your destiny in writing such an amazing life-changing impeccable and necessary book. It may have taken you some time but you made it. Many lives will be changed because of your obedience and desire to help people regardless of their ethnicity. I am very honored to have the opportunity to work side by side with you and watch how you evolve with the spirit of excellence. Every tear that you have shed it was necessary, every night that you laid awake contemplating this powerful book it was necessary, every smile that came across your face during the process of writing this life-changing memoir it was necessary. I look forward to seeing what the Lord has for you to do in the future as you add to this powerful collection of words.

Gracefully yours,

Prophetess Cynthia Bennett

ACKNOWLEDGEMENTS

To my children James, Desiree, Destiny, Joshua, my husband James
E. Smith, my 1st granddaughter Valintina and to all my
grandchildren to come for all their support.
To my Archbishop Willie and Pastor Rhonda Bolden for their love,
support, and prayers. Also, for Pastor Rhonda's encouragements and
the nudge so that this book can be birthed (because it has been lying
dormant for over 20 years.)
To my sisters Mattie Burr, Shamia Williams, and my brother
Johnny Burr Jr., thank you for always being in my corner and for all
of your prayers.
To my spiritual godparents, James and Vinest Jackson thank you for
all your love, support, and encouragement.
To all those who prayed for me, spoke my book into fruition,
family, church members, friends, and to you for your support.
Men, Women, Boys & Girls, it is never too late to do anything- even
to write a book.
Many blessings to you all!

DEDICATION

I dedicate this first book to the Lord on high, who guided me and helped me to write it.

A thank you to my Parents: Johnny and Mary Ann Burr for being a strong man and woman, raising me in the admiration of the Lord, and for never giving up on me.

I also dedicate this book to my Archbishop Willie and Pastor Rhonda Bolden for having faith in me to reach my goal of publishing.

FORWARD

By **Pastor Rhonda Bolden**

In the midst of current events in the world and life's challenging times, this powerful Book, "Uplifting Poetry to Rejuvenate the Hurting Soul," has been birthed through Rowena Smith to bring LIFE back to your LIFE!

You will realize and greatly enjoy, as I have, her gift of writing, and it will be evident why you are here now with its pages open ready to Receive. These inspiring Words from Rowena's heart and soul will bring light in the dark hidden areas of your life and help you begin to radiate and glow with excitement for your future.

The Word of God says in Psalms 45:1 "My heart is overflowing with a beautiful thought! I will write a lovely poem to the King, for I am as full of words as the speediest writer pouring out his story." (TLB) "Beautiful words stir my heart. I will recite a lovely poem about the king, for my tongue is like the pen of a skillful poet, a ready Writer!" (NLT/NKJV)

These words of life are sure to elevate your Mind/Body/Spirit to another dimension above your circumstances and cares of life. You will receive Divine Inspiration to give you Hope instead of despair, Joy instead of mourning and Peace in the midst of your current storm, which Will Not Last. When we experience tragedies, we forget that they are just temporary setbacks and not permanent.

"Uplifting Poetry to Rejuvenate the Hurting Soul," will catapult and uplift your soul to become a better person to begin to "Soar like never before and remind you that You are Wise and, on the Rise, and will not be denied!"

Get ready to be raised up, to improve, to be inspired and stirred up, to be edified and touched in your soul right where you need it. I pray that it will even AWAKEN the Writer in you, so you can also be a blessing to world as our spiritual daughter Rowena Smith is to us and so many.
Enjoy Your Journey reading this masterpiece and living your LIFE to the fullest for the Glory of God. God Bless!

PASTOR RHONDA BOLDEN
Fort Wayne, Indiana
www.RhondaBolden.com

CONTENTS

ACKNOWLEDGEMENTS 4

DEDICATION..5

FORWARD..6

POEMS OF HURT 1

POEMS OF LONELINESS 13

POEMS FOR FORGIVENESS 19

POEMS FOR ENDURANCE... 24

POEMS FOR ENCOURAGEMENT.. 30

POEMS FOR *LOVE*.. 42

POEMS FOR STRENGTH.. 50

INSPIRATIONAL QUOTES.. 58

Poems of HURT

FRIENDSHIP

The poem **Friendship** was inspired when a close friend, who became my sister, turned on me for no reason. She became jealous, stopped talking to me, blocked me on social media and when I would see her in public she would act as though nothing was wrong. I began to realize it was not her, it was the enemy trying to destroy our friendship and cause confusion. I had to realize that people can just be so caught up in life, that I started looking with my spiritual eyes and began praying for her. Did she ever come around and did I forgive her? "YES" I did and yes, she did come round and apologized.

FRIENDSHIP

We all want to be friends!

Do we really know the meaning of a friendship?

A Friend is someone that will support you till the end,

Someone you can depend on in the time of need,

Someone who keeps everything in confidence,

Someone that has a disagreement

But always knows how to

Be the bigger person and say sorry and let it go.

A friend will never backstab you,

Nor betray you,

Steal from you,

Get Jealous of you,

Try to outdo you.

If you ever have a friend like that, you better hold to them tight.

A friend sticketh closer than a brother.

Proverbs 18:24

GET BACK UP AGAIN

When you've done all you can,

Times we have lost the battle, but

Get back up and walk in the war... bruised, battered, hurt, and

wounded.

PEACE

The poem **Peace** may be my deepest poem. It came from a place in my life at a time of trouble, hurt, pain, and a time where I thought God had abandoned me. I lost my two best friends, my support system, the ones who I knew without a shade of a doubt loved me- my parents. My whole world turned upside down. I fell into a deep depression. I felt all alone. I walked away from the church and every hurting thing filled my mind. I felt like I was in quicksand, and I felt there was no hope for me. I struggled to get back in church, hating how they treated me. I eventually, slowly started back attending church, but it was more of a painted smile on my face and hiding behind a mask. I knew I had to get a grip on my life because I was spiraling out of control, I would overeat. I felt my heart hardening. I didn't want to be around people. I was losing trust in people- mainly church folks. I began hating myself to the point I didn't want to live and hated looking in the mirror. But, by God's grace, I am still here and I have grown to love, forgive, and He has filled that void in my life. Things may not be all fine and I still have problems, but I know it's nothing too hard for God to handle and I can trust him in ALL things, no matter what the situation may be.

PEACE

At times we all look for a peace of mind.

Just to make it through the day.

Some of us think we have it all together but there is no rest and no

end

To our trouble and pain.

I'm here to tell you I've been there.

Never ending troubles, so many heart aches after heart aches,

Mentally abused, raped in my own home, the feeling of being

unloved,

Attempted and thoughts of suicide, mistreated by love ones, hurted

by

Church folks, betrayed by so called friends, left with a void when

both

Of my parents passed away, the feeling of loneliness when someone

is

Right there next to me, and hiding behind a smile but drowning in

my own

Tears on the inside. Wondering will it ever end and wondering will

Someone saved me from myself and this hurtful misery.

When I accepted Jesus in my life completely

I found a peace that passes all understanding.

I found rest and my purpose

Because Jesus handle all my pain, troubles, hurts, disappointment,

Renewed my mind, circumsized my heart, wiped my tears away, filled my

Voids, and gave me hope,

You too can have this only if you truly accept and let him in.

Jeremiah 31:16, Revelation 21:4, Philippians 4:7

SHATTERED GLASS

A broken heart is like a shattered glass.
Pieces shifting each way, swept up and thrown away.
Only not to be repaired but once it hits the trash the repair process
begins.
A process of healing and restoration begins because our brokenness
was never meant to break us but to make us stronger, wiser, and a
living testimony to help someone else.

TIK-TOK

The **Tick-Tock** poem was written at a time in my life, before I got saved and accepted the Lord Jesus Christ in my life. It lets you know our anger from past, present, and future hurts can cause a lot of damage to us and others. But when we allow the Lord to take control, it will be much easier to go through it. There was a time where I had no self-control with my anger. I held so much on the inside that it often came out in a way that wasn't good. I was the nicest person till someone made me mad. It's like it triggered the hurt and pain. I felt like I was not going to let anyone hurt me again so walls started forming around me, blocking feelings and emotions out. The anger came from a lot of hurt, pain, and abuse over the years. Being such a private person, I didn't really share my problems. So, I held them in which now I know that's not a good thing to do. The Lord placed someone in my life that I could talk with and trust. Now that I am saved is everything perfect? No it isn't, I still get hurt by people, I still go through problems, and my prayers don't get answered right away but that doesn't mean He doesn't hear us. With the Lord, I'm learning how to channel my hurts and control my anger. I started helping hurting women and it has now become a passion.

TICK-TOCK

Not having self-control is like a ticking time bomb boiling under

pressure waiting to explode.

Causing debris to scatter abroad

hurting innocent bystanders.

Who is to blame for this mass destruction?

Could it be the circumstances that try to control me?

Could it be the past on how it hurts and cuts so deep?

Could it be that person who caused so much pain and left the

stinger penetrating in my heart and brain?

Full of misery... searching for someone to extinguish this flame.

Tick tock! Tick tock! Tick tock!

Time is running out!!

What substance can be doused?

Who can saturate the tip of this ticking bomb?

Flames blazing and particles boiling

ready to burst out from this unbearable pressure.

How can I contain these uncontrollable feelings?

Help Me!!!!

Peace, be still!!

I can't and won't put more on you than you can bear!

You are more than a conqueror

In a still soft whisper!

Strengthen, by every word that flowed down in my soul

Stabilizing the flame instead of extinguishing it and

leading me to self-control over my own self destruction.

The poem Wise Woman was an inspirational for women to know that they are more than just women. We are important, we matter, we have authority over our TEMPORARY CIRCUMSTANCES, we are beautiful, we do not have to cry sad tears, and no matter what we went through or going through we will always come out on top. If we as women allow God to be head of our life it would be much easier; will trouble still come "YES" but with Christ, it is such a smoother transition when we have those hard times.

Wise WOMAN

Woman of Excellence!

Your time is now!!

Woman of honor, grace, peace, and love.

Stand up!

Hold your head up high.

Wipe your tears, dry your eyes.

No more weeping or mourning.

Your time has come.

Your better has arrived.

Spread your wings and soar high as an Engle.

Soar freely as you are within.

Woman of courage!

Can't you see all the fears, hurt, pain you have conquered and the despair you have overcame?

Can't you see that your walk is full of virtue and authority?

Your arms are strong and made to withstand the task that you face day after day.

Woman of Strength

Though you may have struggles within the enemy will never win.

Virtuous woman you are

Beauty and love dwells on the inside and out

No flowing river can compare itself to the compassion, confidence,

and anointing that surrounds you.

Take no thought of tomorrow for it will take care of itself.

Woman of honor, grace, peace, and love.

Stand up!

Hold your head up high.

Free you are and free you will stay.

Woman of Excellence!

WOMAN of EXCELLENCE!!!!

Get up!

Hold your head up and shine

Wise Woman

Your time is now!

Poems of LONELINESS

EYES

Some say the eyes are the window of someone's soul.

Look into my eyes

Can you see a world that lies within me?

A world of challenges;

Challenges that seems so impossible to overcome,

A world of loneliness

As though lifelessness lies within me

Someone's soul that appears to be lost and can't be found.

As a flowing river of tears drowning me and leaving me gasping for

air.

A hidden place to hide all of my hurts and pains.

Take a look in the mirror and see what lies behind the eyes of your

soul

Then release it to the Lord from which cometh our help.

Then and only then shall your healing begin.

STAND

Married woman,

about to get married

and those who are going through.

Always remember there is a God that is above every problem and

situation.

You can soar higher than anyone can ever image.

Remember everything has a reason for happening.

Our problems come to make us stronger,

not to fall weak for them.

Stand strong woman of strength.

Stand. It's only temporary.

(1 Peter 5:10)

SURVIVOR

Dry your tears, no more weeping, you are not alone. Your time is now!!!

You have overcome; you have survived and weathered the most treacherous storm!!

The pieces to your life are coming together to form a new and transformed you.

You are the victory of every one of your circumstances of yesterday, today, and tomorrow.

You are the strength over every one of your adversities of the past, present, and future.

Mishaps, hurts, pain, trauma, disappointments, depression, sickness, diseases, and suicidal thoughts no longer control you.

You are a Survivor!

TIME

Time is moving as there will be no tomorrow

Second to minute

Minutes to hours

Where has time gone?

Day to night

Months to years

In a blink of an eye, time has done come and gone

Moving as if it's a speeding train, racing so it wouldn't be late.

Season to season

Time moves as if there is no longer twelve hours, but only seconds.

Holiday to holiday

Time makes it seem all but a short memory.

Oh my where has time gone?

WHEN I WAS LOST

Lonely, cold, and dark as night!

Laying here as if death is standing beside me.

In and out, In and out'

My mind wonders as though the world is coming to an end.

Am I going to live or am I going to die?

What do I have to live for?

Who wants me?

Help!

I cry out in the midst of my sickness.

No one answers.

Dead silence entertains me.

Then a soft laughter I hear off in a distance.

Louder and louder it gets! Who are you, what are you?

Death it replied!

Is this how you feel? Lonely, cold, and dark as night?

No reply at all given.

With a blink of an eye, darkness was all gone and there before me

was a bright light.

Now I see clearly what lies ahead spiritually for me.

I see destiny, life, purpose, as an overcomer of my deepest fears.

I am found

I'm no longer lost.

Poems for FORGIVENESS

AT PEACE

When your mind is at peace, you are not affected by what people think or say about you and there is no restless thinking.
We will not be moved by difficulties and will be able to maintain clear judgment in all situations.

DISAPPOINTMENT

Disappointment is like a friend that we all had before.

It sticks to you like a bee to a flower, searching for nectar and

pollen in the spring.

A mother protecting her young.

A musician who finds his music from his soul.

Even though it's a friend you would never want to keep around.

Because all disappointment is filled with hurt and pain.

Hardship ending up with a heart shattered in many pieces.

Undercover it is

Showing up uninvited.

Trying to steal my joy, peace, and happiness.

The same way you tried to come in.

The same way you must leave

because we are

Strong, Wise women!!

As we stand tall with our head held high and looking disappointed

in the face.

You will never win

Weeping may endure for a night, but joy always comes in the

morning.

DON'T ALLOW PEOPLE

*Don't allow people's chain of refusal to forgive, jerk you around.
God is a forgiving God.
We don't have to carry our mistakes. So, why allow someone to
carry them and hold them over our head as a pawn. We are not a
pawn shop. But, we are children of the Most High, so we need to
pray for them, show the love of Christ, and not judge them.
Lord, help us today to forgive anyone that has wrong us with a
sincere heart and mind. Allow the other person to have a sincere
heart and mind as well, so that we will not be stagnated in our walk
with you.*

TWO WRONGS

Only you can make your peace last.

If you wrong someone, tell them that you're sorry.

If someone has wronged you, forgive them.

For the bible says: forgive them for they know not what they do.

Release them, for it's not worth having unforgiveness.

That person can't make you, nor can they break you.

Live your life,

Don't let someone live yours.

Matthew 6:14; Mark 11:25; Luke 23:34

Poems for ENDURANCE

BATTLE

My brother and sister

When this life comes at you like a flood.

Drowning you to a point of your last breath,

Just know that no weapon formed against you shall prosper.

Whatever you may be going through

Or

What someone may be doing to discourage you,

Just know God will fight your battle.

The battle is not yours.

It's the Lord's.

DON'T GIVE UP

When things don't seem to work out;

And everytime you turn around something's going wrong,

As if you are the enemy

Feeling as if you're climbing a mountain

And never going to make it to the top.

When you do make it, there appears another mountain blindsiding

your victory.

Holding on by a string.

Don't give up. You can't give up.

Cause trouble doesn't last always.

There is a beam of light at the end of every dark long tunnel.

LOOK BACK

Either we trust that the Lord will Guide and Provide, or we just
simply don't.
If we trust the Lord to handle our everyday situations
Ask yourself why?
Why do we look back at our situation like Lot's wife written before
our very eyes in
Genesis 19:26?
We can only imagine Lot's wife looking back on Sodom and
Gomorrah in disbelief, worry, fear, frustration, disappointment, and
curiosity.
How many times must our spirit turn into a pillar of salt?
How many times must our spirit turn into a pillar of salt?
Why must we look back at the problems and situations that we have
given to God?
He said he will take care of our every need.
But we take it right back with our Worry, fear, Frustration,
disappointment, and curiosity.
Lord, why can't we see that we have become stagnated spiritually
and or spiritually crippled?
I ask once again, how many times must our spirit turn into a pillar
of salt for looking back?

ONLY TIME WILL TELL

Are you real or fake?

Some people may ask or even wonder

Not knowing or understanding how you gave your life for us

Until we actually accept you as our personal savior.

The many times you came through for us,

Blessings after blessings,

Miracles after miracles,

The many prayers you answered,

The many times you carried us under your wings of safety,

The many times we were hurt, misused, and cried you embraced us

in your bosom,

In the many times we needed you the most and you said it will be ok

my child.

Sending your comforter time after time when we felt we couldn't

make it another day.

Times you felt so far away when you were right there all the time.

So wrapped up in our own problems to the point they tried to blind

side us in seeing how you are closer to us than we could ever

imagine.

So how can some ask are you real or are you fake?

Only time will tell!!

John 1:1-14, John 3:16, Romans 3:10-18, Romans 5:12

ROSE

There once was a rose that was sweet to the smelling and beautiful for all to see. One day it was cut and put in water and as the days went by the rose got less attention eventually it came to the point where it wasn't worth looking at any more so the person threw it away. Someone came along and picked it up, knowing what to do with it. In doing so he examined it for a sign of life. As he starts cutting the base of the stem, he sees It has green underneath the brown looking stem. A smile came on his face as he proceeded with the next step by taking all the old leaves off and cleaning it up a bit. Wrapping it up in a wet newspaper and putting it in a dark moist place in his house. Weeks went by and then the man went to check on the stem one day much to his surprise there were roots beginning to grow on it. He then planted it in his yard and a month went by one morning he woke up to a lot of noise he then began looking out the window and saw many people in his yard. The man went to see, there was a beautiful rose in the middle of his yard more beautiful than before. One man said, I once had a rose like this. Not realizing it was the same Rose he threw away a long time ago.

Never count anyone out Jesus can clean up anyone and make them into something better than they were before

Poems for
ENCOURAGEMENT

CHANGE

Time after time we find ourselves doing the same thing over and

over

Going in circles as though it's a merry go round.

When will it stop?

When will the change come?

Look deep down to the depths of your soul.

Tell yourself I need a change.

The change starts with you.

Once you let Jesus in your heart.

Allow him to be your personal saver.

That's the biggest change anyone can ever make.

Will you make that change?

DEAR READER

Dear Reader Is a poem to relax, let everything go, clear your mind of all negativity, and focus on yourself- mind, body and soul.

DEAR READER

Dear Reader,

Close your eyes

Imagine yourself standing in that inner place.

Relax.

Imagine yourself standing near the seashore

Hear the claim of the waves as they slowly hit the standing shore.

The softest sound as though you have a seashell to your ear.

Imagine yourself soaring high above the earth as an eagle.

Soaring so high no one or anything can touch you.

A cool crisp breeze whispering past your ears.

A soft wind blows through your hair.

Image yourself being free

From all memories

Freer than a lion roaming free in the wild land.

Dear reader, you are free!

I AM AT PEACE

I am at peace in my mind, body, soul, my heart, my home, my job,
my marriage,
with my kids, and with people in my life.
Lord, I pray whoever reads this that the peace I feel will overflow
on them and all that surrounds them.
I bind frustration, aggravation, irritation, and distractions.
I lose peace right now over their mind, homes, marriages,
jobs, finances, families, and people in Jesus name amen.

JOY

Joy can break chains

Joy can mend broken hearts

Joy can brighten a room on its dimmest day

Joy can reunite unforgiveness to forgiveness

Joy is tender and fragile but yet remains strong when misused.

Joy withstands every battle.

KINDNESS

Kindness is like a medicine that circulates through my veins
Shielding me from all matter of poisons that tries to destroy my
happiness, peace, and joy.
Kindness has become a part of my soul, a part of me.
I've become contagious as it flows from the crown of my head to the
soles of my feet.
With every touch it passes as though it's an uncontrollable wild fire
demolishing every unkind spirit that stands in its way and
maneuvers around it's every tactic.
Who am I? I am Kindness.

MIRROR

As I look gazing in the mirror.

Who do I see?

Is it me or is someone pretending to be me?

As I look into her eyes they seem as though I'm looking through a window

Seem as if she is trapped

Yelling, crying, hurting and trying to find a way out.

I see others standing in the mirror seeing her calm and steady

As the cool breeze on a warm summer day.

Peace surrounds her as though nothing is wrong.

But why can't anyone see her

Yelling, crying, hurting and trying to find a way out to let go of this hindrance?

The endurance to stand, know that the Lord's peace is with her and her heart doesn't need to be troubled neither afraid.

John 4:27

MOTHER

Mothers take your child by their hand, little or big.

Tell them that you love them with a big hug.

It's best to do it when they are young because they grow up so fast.

Faster than you can blink your eyes.

Thank God for them for they are truly a gift from Him.

Always remember there are many who want them but can't have

any.

From one mother to another;

Always love and forgive because we were also once a child.

OPPORTUNITY

People cannot give us peace.

Our peace comes from God and Him alone.

When he gives us peace we are able to operate in his will gracefully.

When the world offers us peace it's a false peace that is temporary and it can be taken back when given.

Having you feeling uneasy at times but with the Lord's peace we have an opportunity to have it everlasting.

PEACE LIKE A STREAM

Peace is like a flowing stream flowing smoothly over every rock and
stone.
Maneuvering around obstacles; gracefully standing in its way.
Always flowing forward and never looking back.
Making soothing music as it flows relaxing my every thought and
resting in its every peace.

QUEEN

The poem **Queen** was inspired by my Archbishop and Pastor. They call us rich Queens all the time. I never saw myself as a queen until I met them. But we all are queens, we are all royalty in the eye sight of the Lord, We have to look beyond the mirror, the negativity people say about us and know that God sees NO flaws because we all are flawless in his eyesight.

QUEEN

Queen, whatever you're going through

Or if you're not sure of yourself

Look up in a mirror and see the strength within you

The wonderful graceful woman that you are.

You are stronger than you think.

No more crying, depression, hurting, and pretending!

You are a queen!

So, rise above yourself and fix your crown!

This is a new day.

Rejoice and be glad in it.

Open your heart my queen.

Trouble doesn't last always.

Psalm 30:5

STRANGER TO A KING

How could this be?

I know everything about you.

Down to the smell of your cologne!

At times we would stand side by side.

Hand and hand, face to face!

We would look into each other's eyes

Staring into each other's souls!

Waiting on my king!

Never for one second did I allow my thought to wonder

But how could I? You're the one I love.

Waiting on my king!

Moved by your every word!

Satisfied with your every touch;

Swept away with all your lavished gift,

And your genuine compassion.

How could this be?

I fell into the arms of a king.

And now he is my husband, friend, and lover.

Wait on the lord to send you your king!

Poems for *LOVE*

LOVE FLOWS

Love is like a river

It never stops flowing through our veins

It circulates through our body always returning back to our heart.

LOVE

Love is a word with so much power, strength and control.

Only one can imagine how one can be hypnotized by the word

called love.

Moved by its warmth,

Comforted by its every touch

Mesmerized by its every words

When it's near safety surrounds me.

All my trust and secrets lie within it.

My heart is wrapped in locks and chains.

All over a word called love.

What is love? Who is love? God is love!

NO GREATER LOVE

No other love can compare to the love that we encounter on a daily

basis.

A Love that's so strong that the strongest man can't rip it away from

anyone!

A Love that forgives all our wrongs!

A Love with forgiveness that is never used as a weapon to destroy or

tear us down!

A Love that caused Him to lay his life down for me and you so that

we can live.

What greater Love is that?

A Love that sustains you and I!

A Love that we don't deserve but yet it remains the same!

A Love that comforts us daily when hurt and pain tries to destroy

us!

A Love where his mercy endures forever!

A Love where his grace is sufficient for you and I!

A Love that restores broken hearts!

A Love that never hurts but only heals and encourages!

A Love only given from the Lord above

What is his name?

Jesus, Master, Son of God, Lamb of God, El Shaddai(God

Almighty).

Greater love hath no man than this, that a man lay down is life for

his friend.

John 15:13

THAT NIGHT

That night of love and passion

Our bodies lying side by side

Your fingers ran through my hair

Your eye's connecting with mine

Your lips kissed my lips sending chills down my spine.

Gently touching my breast as we made love

That night

Aw that wonderful night of passion

Wanting it to never end

Your every stroke, touch, and kiss entangled me.

Making me only yearn for more!

Yearn for the true passion that lies deep within my husband, my king,

heart, mind, body, and soul.

That night!

THE WIND

As I sit under this old oak tree minding my own;

Here comes this wind caressing my face.

Strong and mighty;

But soft to the touch!

I ask, do you know me?

But a howl is the only response.

As the wind passes my lips.

feels as though I was kissed.

It combs through my hair.

and blows my sun dress side to side as if it's trying to seduce me.

I ask again do you know me?

Once again only a howl in response.

And then it was gone.

Only for a moment the wind was something special.

Once again, it's just me sitting under this old oak tree.

TRUTH

True friends help each other find the way to the truth;

The truth is Jesus!

This is for you my friend,

Jesus is waiting at the door.

Will you open it and let him in?

All you have to do is ask him to forgive you of all your sins;

Come into your heart.

Believe He died on the cross

Was raised on the third day!

To save you and me from death

Lord I take you as my personal saver.

Help guide me to live for you in Jesus name I pray, Amen.

May your walk with Jesus be blessed!

1 Corinthians 15:3-4. 1 John 5:16, 1 John 1:9

YOU ARE

You are the reason my heart beats.

You are the reason why I want to get up in the morning and go to bed at night.

You are the reason why I go but always find my way back to you.

You are the reason why I am the woman I am today. You helped me build my strength, our family, and my values.

You are the reason I am a Queen and you're my King even in the times it doesn't feel like it.

You are the reason why I love you so much because you put up with my flaws and problems. Times you could have walked away but you stayed and tried to fight a little longer. For that I know deep down your Love for me is pure even through the tears we both have shed through the years.

You are a man of God, even though you may have flaws as well. With God on our side, flaws can always be flawless. Stay strong for me and I will stay strong for you. I Thank God for you always and forever!!! My KING

Poems for STRENGTH

Foolish wonder is a poem based on the adversities we face in life and how at times they try to bring us down to a point in our life where we cannot function. But in that one split second, the Lord reminds us that we are stronger than we think because he tells us that no weapon formed against us shall prosper. We are more than conquerors, by His stripes we are healed, and He will never leave us nor forsake us. For that I am grateful, and it gives me strength to go on.

FOOLISH WONDER

You thought you had me fooled.
How foolish can you be?
You tried to destroy me but I'm still standing.
Foolish wonder
I'm stronger than you can imagine.
You tried to trick me, break me,
Lie to me,
Use me and
Devour me.
You foolish wonder,
I see right through you.
I'm stronger than you could ever imagine.

ME!

As I look into the depths of your eyes

Entering through the window

Of your soul, Who do I see?

Who is this extraordinary queen?

Who is this woman that captivates everyone that surrounds her?

Who is this woman that can stand under tremendous amount of

pressure and can carry the weight of the world on her shoulders so

gracefully?

Who is this woman that can love above every hurt, pain, mishaps

and yet her love is pure as gold?

Her smile and beauty are forever radiating.

Her personality is a natural born leader, always striving for

greatness to be in others.

Her walk is full of strength, love, peace, joy and faithfulness.

Her crown glistens and shines bright as she wears it exquisitely

well.

Her devastations have never demolished nor diminished her

purpose because she still stands, she walks in authority and holds

her head high.

Though she may feel her destiny is out of reach at times, in her

heart she knows with faith, grace, mercy and guidance, The lord

will direct her every step.

Who is she?

What is this queen name?

Me!!!! That is her name and I wear it well

RAINDROPS FROM HEAVEN

Raindrops falling from heaven

Knocking on my windowpane

Making music as if an angel is singing a soft melody to me.

Where only I can hear?

Raindrops from heaven

Drip, drip to the rhythm of my heartbeat.

Fallin into a trance as though I've been hypnotized!

Rain drops from heaven

Smoothing to my soul

I sign from the heaven above

That every tear drop that falls from my eyes

Is wiped away from the Lord above.

SAFE HAVEN

No more weeping and no more mourning.
There is a safe haven in the midst of all your tears.

A STRONG WOMAN is a poem that I wrote when I was going through a hard time in my life, my marriage, kids, finances, and just everyday life problems. But with much praying and waiting, the Lord allowed me to see the strength that was on the inside of me- which was our Lord and Savior Jesus Christ. I know if he lives in me, I can do all things through Christ who strengthens me.

Philippians 4:13

STRONG WOMAN

I am a strong woman
Stronger than any mighty warrior
My strength is within me.
I am a strong woman
I overcome every and all circumstances that may try
To overcome me.
I am a strong woman
A woman that stands tall and proud.
Fierce as any lion.
I am a strong woman
Who is more precious than diamonds and pearls
I am a strong woman
A woman who fights every battle

tried and weary

But yet I stand and win!

I am a strong woman!

WITHIN ME

Who am I sitting here?

Drowning in my own tears

Gasping for air like it's my last breath.

left here to drown in my own tears

Fighting to stay afloat!

Praying for my savior to come to save me.

Fighting the enemy lies, feeling like they're overtaking

me.

Holding on with all the strength that is within me

Come to realize I'm not

alone my strength and savior lives within me.

1 Corinthians 3:16

WOMAN OF STRENGTH

Woman of strength

Why are you so discouraged?

Your tears flow as though there is a never-ending river.

Woman of strength

Why are you so weary?

Your smile was once a smile of hope.

Now hope turned into despair.

Woman of strength

Why are you so weak?

Your stand and your words were stronger than the mightiest

man.

Now your strength has become a weakness.

Woman of strength

Why won't you stand?

INSPIRATIONAL QUOTES

by: **Rowena Smith**

A KEY TO HAVING PEACE

A key to having peace! We must change our thinking, refuse to entertain negative gossip, rebuke the negative thoughts that the enemy tries to bring us and not ponder or play with them.
Lord, I speak peace over each one of us. Give us the discernment and will power to cast down all imaginations that the enemy may bring to our mind that is not of you. Help us to refocus our mind and become more spiritual minded. In Jesus Name! Amen

❖ ❖ ❖

ADVERSITY

Just because a rose has thorns, does that stop us from buying them or giving them to a loved one? Just because we have attacks and storms in our lives, we don't have to give up nor let it defeat us.

❖ ❖ ❖

AT TIMES WE FEEL BROKEN

In the times we feel broken beyond repair just know that there is someone who can put us back together again.
Thank God for a Potter who molds us back together better than we were before.
Jeremiah 18: 2-6

BEGIN SHAKING

Sometimes people that are not meant to be in our destiny will fall off like a dead leaf all on their own. So begin shaking and watch them fall away.

❖ ❖ ❖

COME FORWARD

It's time to come out of the grave clothes and come forward. The Lord is calling us out of the grave. Let the bandages of hurt, pain, worries, depression, persecution, despair, frustration, disappointment, unforgiveness, and all the cares of this world fall off because the Lord paid the ultimate price for all of us. We carry unnecessary dead weight when we do not have to.
The bandages had to come off Lazarus when the Lord called him forward out of the grave.
Even death could not hold Lazarus.

John 11:41-44

❖ ❖ ❖

DON'T HAND IT OVER

The devil cannot steal your joy.
But you can hand it over to him by
allowing situations, people, unforgiveness, anger, and attitude control you.
Never let anything or anyone bring you out of character.
The Lord said vengeance is mine and I will repay. ***Romans 12:19***

A soft answer turns away wrath. **Prov 15:1**

If your enemy is hungry, give him bread to eat, and if he is thirsty,

give him water to drink.

Proverbs 25:21-23

❖ ❖ ❖

DREAMS

In life you must be careful who you share your dreams with. Either they will be for you, against you, support you, or walk away. Stand strong because God makes no mistakes. They were never supposed to be in your vision anyway. Step out on faith! Have your way Jesus.

❖ ❖ ❖

DROP THE WEIGHT

Stop carrying unnecessary weight.

If it is not strengthening, edifying us or someone

It is useless!!

Why be miserable behind closed doors when you don't have to?

EXPECTING

If you are expecting a blessing don't miss it by overlooking the small one.

That one could lead you to the greater one.

FAINT NOT

Only if we are patient and faint not, in the end will we reap the benefits. The beginning will determine our ending.

We can never count anyone out because at times we all fall short and have a chance to get it together.

❖ ❖ ❖

FLOODGATES

We do not have to wait till the end of the year for the floodgates of Heaven to open.

They can open at this very moment.

Just worship the Lord.

❖ ❖ ❖

FULL CONTROL

The Lord has full control of EVERYTHING big or small.

So set your life in cruise control mode, leave it there permanently, and just relax.

Luke 12:22-26 Isaiah 41:10

GOD SEES EVERYTHING

God sees everything whether you try to hide it in your mind or your heart. Eventually it is going to come to the light.

❖ ❖ ❖

GOD WILL SEE US THROUGH

God will see us through anything. All we have to do is stand still, have faith, and trust in his every word. God does not start something and does not finish it. A setback does not mean it is over. Just evaluate the situation and hear what God is saying to you at that moment.

Thank you, Lord!!

❖ ❖ ❖

GRATEFUL

Be grateful for what we have, be thankful for where God has brought us from, and where He is elevating us to.

Growth is necessary!!

HE KNOWS

The enemy knows how to dress as well.

Be careful who you let in your life.

❖ ❖ ❖

HOLD ON

When we go through a storm, we will be tossed each and

every way, but when we come out, we are all intact. I am a living

Witness.

Hallelujah, thank you Jesus.

Hold on!!!

❖ ❖ ❖

HUMBLE

Humbling ourselves is not a sign of weakness or defeat.

In doing so, we never know whose life it might change or save.

I WIN

Everything that is attached to me WILL WIN. This is my season! I speak it into the atmosphere. Despite what it may look like right now. God has the last say so. In Jesus name! Amen!!

❖ ❖ ❖

IN THE MIDST OF IT ALL

In the midst of it ALL. Let us lift our hands to worship and let our soul cry out Hallelujah.
The enemy has NO POWER / AUTHORITY.

❖ ❖ ❖

TEMPORARY

During our temporary going through, take a moment to see the finished victory (Jesus) and not the process. Do not let the enemy blindside you with distractions.

IN YOUR TIMING

In your timing Lord because the outcome will be better and greater.

I do not mind waiting on you Lord!!

❖ ❖ ❖

OBEY

It is better to obey the Lord then to be blindsided by the enemy.

Do not ever let anything hinder the work of the Lord.

Our purpose is very important.

❖ ❖ ❖

IT IS NOT GREENER

Just because someone else's grass appears to be greener on the other side, we must tend too & exam our own brown spots because theirs could be artificial grass.

IT IS NOT OVER

God is setting the stage. Be ready and do not allow pettiness (distractions from the enemy) make you miss it.
Activate faith, obedience, love, & forgiveness!

❖ ❖ ❖

BEWARE

Just because the wheat and tares grow together doesn't mean everything and everyone is for you. The enemy knows how to disguise himself also and so do people.

❖ ❖ ❖

DON'T LET IT BE TOO LATE

Life is too short, forgive quickly and love unconditionally.

LIFE

Sometimes you must look at life from a different angle to see your purpose.

It may hurt momentarily but the ending results are a cure-all.

❖ ❖ ❖

LORD I NEED YOU

Lord I need you for everything seen and unseen, known and unknown. Help me, I am sinking in my own quicksand. Save me from myself, Lord Jesus.

❖ ❖ ❖

LIVE CYCLE

Your love is like a river,

It never stops flowing through my veins,

It circulates through my body always returning back to my heart.

MAKING ME STRONGER

The enemy is a thief, liar, and robber. He tries to persuade or entice us to hand over our joy, peace, happiness, love, and blessings to him by using our problems and situations against us. Little does he know? Our problems and situations come to make us stronger, not to break us, We are being built up for a testimony to help someone else.

❖ ❖ ❖

MIRROR

I, me, we, and Jesus are my cheerleader. Look in the mirror and kiss yourself. See your beauty. You do not need lip service from others.

❖ ❖ ❖

DISASTER

Just because disaster may take place around us, that doesn't mean our story is over. We're stronger than we think & trouble doesn't last always.

NEVER ALLOW

Never allow someone to take you out of your character and pull you into their misery.

❖ ❖ ❖

NO COMMUNICATION

No prayer life = No communication with the Lord. Meaning; your Lifeline is severed off. No personal relationship with him, you're not thinking of others to pray for them, no covering your children or your family, no guidance, wisdom, strength, and blessings being missed. Prayer is a vital part of our lives.

❖ ❖ ❖

NOT JUST A WORD

Don't just listen to the word.
Seek and receive the revelation in it.
It pours out powerful wisdom & knowledge.

NOTHING

There is nothing too hard for God. He has a purpose & a plan for each and every one of us. We just have to hold on in the midst of our hardest times, stand our ground when the enemy tries to shake us, swim and not drown in our own tears, and let go of unforgiveness quickly.

❖ ❖ ❖

ONLY TEMPORARILY

Birth pains are only temporarily. Therefore, trouble doesn't last always

1 Peter 5:10

Hold on a little longer. Victory is coming!

❖ ❖ ❖

PAST AND FUTURE

Living in the past only shortens your present and your future. Let it be a testimony not a sob story.

PROCESS

People are moved out of our lives for a reason, replaced with a ram in the bush. Even dead branches have to be pruned for new growth to reach its full potential.

❖ ❖ ❖

PRAY FOR PEOPLE

If people can't forgive you for past mistakes pray for them and just know God forgives.

❖ ❖ ❖

POWER, PRAYER AND WORSHIP

Never underestimate the POWER of Prayer and Worship. They're powerful tools if you know how to use them.

RIVER OF PEACE

My heart is so filled with joy and love. I feel a river of peace flowing

through me.

Thank you, Lord,

❖ ❖ ❖

GOD'S ORIGINAL

I am God's original,

The only copy

No one like me exists, life is a one-shot deal.

So, enjoy it.

❖ ❖ ❖

STAND STILL

Seasons change for a reason and when there is a shifting in the

atmosphere something is about to happen. Stand still, God is not

finished with us yet!! Thank you Lord!

STILL STANDING

With God I never lack or lose. I can do all things through Christ Jesus that strengthens me. No weapon formed against me shall prosper. I am more than a conqueror. I am the head and not the tail I am above and not beneath. I am who God says I am. Thank you Lord!!

❖ ❖ ❖

SUNSET

How can people say there is no God...? I really like this sunset today. All I see is beauty, love, grace, and peace. That's what I speak over my life and family ... Thank you Jesus. You are so wonderful.

❖ ❖ ❖

THANK YOU

Lord, I thank you for discernment, for growth, to hear your voice, a heart to love people despite their wrong, a heart to forgive, and an urgency to want to live right.

YOU ARE GREAT

The biggest let down in life is regret and wishing you would have.

God created us to be great and with a purpose so let's begin to walk

in it.

❖ ❖ ❖

THE RIVER BANK

The longer you stand on a river bank holding a fishing pole and

never throwing it out, you will never catch anything.

It's never too late to witness to someone.

❖ ❖ ❖

TIME TO SHIFT

Ask yourself, what if God didn't forgive me and held my past against

me?

How would I feel?

It is time for a shift, to move on to another dimension of growth. To

rise above the pain, hurt, and fears. Standing up face to face with

my opposition and boldly saying

YOU WILL NOT DEFEAT ME ANY LONGER because this day I

win.

I am a forgiver, I am Strong, I can do all things and I am the head

& not the tail above and not beneath

Matthew 6: 14-15

WALKING ALONE IS OKAY

Sometimes in life we have to stand alone to see where we are meant to be going.

❖ ❖ ❖

WALK IN IT

You cannot alter God's plan for your life no matter what you do.

❖ ❖ ❖

WEIGHTS AND HURTS

When the weight and hurt of the world tries to bring us down, always remember this scripture.

Proverbs 31:25 KJV

Strength and honor are her clothing; and she shall rejoice in time to come.

WHEN ALL FAILS

When all fails, just stand on the word of God! I will never leave you nor forsake you, No weapon formed against me shall prosper, I won't put more on you than you can bear, Let us not be weary in well doing for in due season we shall reap if we faint not, and I am more than a conqueror.

❖ ❖ ❖

WHEN I CAN'T SAY A WORD

When I can't say a word! Thank you Lord, for understanding my moan, wave offering, tears, and my every thought. There's no one like you.

❖ ❖ ❖

WHERE WOULD WE BE?

Where would we be without God's love? Where would we be if he didn't give us the strength to stand? Where would we be if he didn't help us to love those who do us wrong when the enemy makes people feel like we did something to them and we didn't? Lord thank you... I need you on a daily basis.

YOU HAVE AUTHORITY

Not in vain, the devil is a liar, deceiver and imitator/duplicator NEVER can he be the ORIGINAL (Jesus). Everything we do for the Lord is profitable, to bless others, and bring glory to the most high our Lord and savior Jesus Christ. Thank you Lord!!

❖ ❖ ❖

YOUR KING

We are QUEENS and should be treated as one.
Yes, we have flaws but don't settle for less.
Let the Lord reveal your king.

Have you accepted Jesus Christ in your Life? If not, Please join me in repeating this prayer.

"Dear God,

I know I'm a sinner, and I ask for your forgiveness.

I believe Jesus Christ is Your Son. I believe that He died for my sin and that you raised Him to life.

I want to trust Him as my Savior and follow Him as Lord, from this day forward. Guide my life and help me to do your will.

I pray this in the name of Jesus. Amen."

After reading this book, what are your plans to Rejuvenate YOUR Hurting Soul?

www.ingramcontent.com/pod-product-compliance
Lightning Source LLC
Chambersburg PA
CBHW031224090426
42740CB00007B/694